Gertrude Stein's Salon and Other Legends

Poems

Laurie Byro

BLUE HORSE PRESS REDONDO BEACH, CALIFORNIA 2015

Gertrude Stein's Salon and Other Legends

Laurie Byro

Blue Horse Press
P.O. Box 7000 - 760
Redondo Beach,
California   90277

Cover art: "Gertrude Stein in Pointellism,"
by Michael Byro

Editors: Jeffrey and Tobi Alfier

ISBN   978-0692579190

ACKNOWLEDGMENTS

The author would like to thank the judges and editors of venues where the following poems first appeared, some in earlier forms:

"Blue on Blue Room, Picasso's Soliloquy, (1901)" Honorable Mention, October 2015, *Web Del Sol*, InterBoard Poetry Community

"27 Rue de Fleurus" - 1st Place, April 2015, *Web Del Sol* InterBoard Poetry Community

"The Ghost Visits Gertrude Stein" - *Vincent Van Go-Gogh*, Writers Among Artists, 2013

"Icarus Plays Atlantic City" - *Literary Bohemian*

"The Ghost of Branwell Drinks Bitters" - *Melancholy Hyperbole*

"The Wild Fir" - *The Guardian Unlimited*

"War, Death, Famine" - *The Legendary, Down and Dirty Word*

"Summer Garden" - *The Literary Review*

"Two Doves" - *Triggerfish*, 2nd Place, March 2011, *Web Del Sol* InterBoard Poetry Community

"Walking With Emily Bronte" - *Triggerfish*

"Fanny Godwin and the Monster" - *Triggerfish*

Additionally, a special thanks to Jeff and Tobi Alfier, for believing in my work and this project. Laura M Kaminski (from the Desert Moon Review Workshop) who has made these books possible through endless discussion, editing, and devotion to poetry, a sister. Kathy Owen, for hours on the phone tweaking, ordering, calming and laughing, a true friend. And, Mitchell Geller, who taught me formalism despite my reluctance, and made it easy for me to embrace pantoums, villanelles, and triolets while holding my hand through the dance, my literati comerado.

For Michael and all my reindeer armies,
friends who didn't make it the first time.

Contents

PART II – Other Legends

PART I – Gertrude Stein's Salon

27 Rue de Fleurus

Prying fingers rattle a fastened door,
she left me her face at the house we both lived in.
Attic secrets itch and claw, in the kitchen, endives
cleaved the broth, melon for a soothing end.

She left me her face at the house we both lived in.
Being a genius took all her time.
Cleaved the broth, melon for a soothing end.
Warned the intruders, warmed love's pipe and slippers.

Being a genius took all her time.
Attic secrets itch and claw, in the kitchen, endives
warned the intruders, warmed Love's pipe and slippers.
Prying fingers rattle a fastened door.

A skillet filled with steam, saffron, wife-servant whore.
Outside the house, Godiva silent and ready.
Smells summon vixens to the window, hounds to the door.
Owls begin their forage, a giant throws his marbles of light.

Outside the house, Godiva silent and ready,
Poem is a poem is a poem is a poem.
Owls begin their forage, a giant throws his marbles of light.
In the farthest part of the yard, a dog becomes the bone.

Poem is a poem is a poem is a poem.
Smells summon vixens to the window, hounds to the door.
In the farthest part of the yard, a dog becomes the bone.
A skillet filled with steam, saffron, wife-servant whore.

Rabbits ribs ache from all their blissful hiding.
Afterwards, it is generally a blue or rose period.
Baby artichokes, asparagus tips, bouillabaisse,
Puss ticks off her list, licks froth from her mouth.

Afterwards, it is generally a blue or rose period.
The simmering onion weeps and wafts.
Puss ticks off her list, licks froth from her mouth.
Trees gather around the house, the muffled keening.

The simmering onion weeps and wafts.
Puss ticks off her list, licks froth from her mouth.
Trees gather round the house, the muffled keening.
Afterwards, it is generally a blue or rose period.

The Ghost Visits Gertrude Stein

I have watched you
and the one you call Alice
during the black petals of sleep,
when all hardness leaves your faces.

There is a field of tulips not far
from the town I lived in as a boy,
with ragged dark flowers.
The spongy earth
still makes these strong and odd,
almost devoid of beauty,
similarly different
from their pastel companions.

Most of my companions are whores.
If I want a woman, I give up
the few guilders set aside for bread
or paint—I've taken the one with lice,
with that violet birthmark staining her cheek.

You are husband to her with your lips.
Your woman's body under those suits
you wear, the edges of your petals
give off luminous sparks,
so strangely you make fire.

If you look closely at my paintings,
you will know my women.
Their proud erect beauty,

their heavy-headed grace. Each Iris,
each Sunflower who has turned from us.

Epigraph:

Pussy love, Pussy Love, where have you been?
Have you frightened off darling Ezra or Hem?
Have you pried loose our rustiest sardine of tin?
Pussy love, Pussy Love, where have you been?
Come close to the fire, desire's no sin —
in that blue-Chagall moonlight you blazed like a gem.
Pussy love, Pussy Love, where have you been?
You have frightened off dearest Pablo and Hem.

Sharpening Her Scissors

It gives me great pleasure to hone the blade, to do
the things that bring peace and order to our favorite
pastime, planning the next soirée, making them salivate

for what we have. Go ahead, tell me she is frivolous,
clawing through dirt, bossing worms and sparrows:
a garden is not the real world.

I do the necessary, chop wood or haul stones for her.
Sharpening her kitchen shears is more than an act
of kindness. Today, before they arrived to fill our

parlor with chatter, I compared the hard windfall
apples she lovingly cut to her breasts. I tried to bite
them then in her kitchen. When she winced I reminded

her she liked it and brandished the blades I'd sharpened
with such care, the shears and the knives. I threatened
I would bring the coldness of metal to our bed if

she continued to scowl. The rule, she knew was to fuss
to my liking. She shooed me like a chicken, said
that night's menu would be spoiled if I didn't

leave her to it; she was busy simmering the apples. I felt
I'd been accused of harvesting paradise. The next morning,
I saw her peppering windfalls at the rock wall

I had just completed building for her. Each discarded
apple burst into white flames as it shattered against stone,
each one reaching its mark.

The Parlor Guest

When the angel of death comes to the house to drive them
to the hospital, they are planning a menu. In her famous

black kettle, Puss blanches vegetables for a soothing
reunion, mixes cream and portents, nothing spicy, peasant stock:

Vincent's Potato Eaters, barley and broth. Impossible
to guess what to offer this stranger with the knowing eyes.

They wave him to the sofa to have tea while he waits.
They don't want to overwhelm him with hospitality.

They don't mind freaks. Parlor-guests juggle stories in the air
as if under a circus tent. Gertrude Stein announces she is weary

of death talk. Bullfights, the wars, schnorrers should stop
chewing the gristly fat off some doomed beast. Alice takes

to resisting popping the heads off chickens, other cooks
say wringing their necks improves the quality of the flesh.

She dreads it when they feign life, splattering blood,
but she prefers it to the pop like a wine cork.

She imagines crazed portrait painters, circling
their heads in garlands of poppies. They purse their lips

at this gentleman as he sips in silence, how much longer, must he
bore them to death? Gertrude Stein wonders if he is drinking down

her name. If her image will appear at the bottom of the china cup.
They sit with him well into a sun splattered noon, again

that horrid bullfight raconteur chimes the hours in their heads.
They comfort themselves that this will make a better story.

While Hubbie holds court, Puss has the gift of the spoon.
She fingers the mole on her breast like a rosary, prays

Husband won't ask this one back. This fellow is awkward,
an intruder too comfy on their couch. She suspects

in the morning he'll insist on having an egg from the hen she
just murdered. She couldn't bear to do it correctly,

the way they taught her. The entire drive to the hospital,
she recalls it careening drunkenly in the yard,

spilled blood splaying round the stump of its once handsome
head: a wreath of Picasso red.

A Poem for Pipes

*I can't stand it to think my life is going so fast and I'm not
really living it.*
  - Ernest Hemingway, The Sun Also Rises

Just as we move from ashtray to salon, we rub up
against one another, heat and smoke burning
through our throats. Our rising influence drags
sooty fingers to the clear frame of sunlight.
An opening to set our souls free, to leave these
coffiny-chests into the open air. All
the rustling currents pass through and over
our heads, the hunter stokes us ardently, as if
embracing a whore. He is without guilt as
he suspects there is no harm to our bodies.
The woman assumes a gentler touch, perhaps
thinking this act, a mutual sin. She coaxes the
filling from pouch, persuades the heat to draw
us out. She uses her sultriest mouth, not easy
for this crone indifferent to her sex.
Still the freedom of the open window, we hope
our scent will join the fresh air. The draw
and suck, a means to release our spirits.
Outside are smells more dominant, relative
for the moment. We pass the oily slick
motor scene, fresh banquettes, the pungent summons
of goat cheese warming in the bowl alongside
overripe pear. We are about to wreak havoc on
the sidewalk as we join Sunday strollers. Our ghostly
remains weave around and through. Breath, then
the mist of others, rising from their mouths.

Resemblance

Another genius said you would become your portrait, age
into your rivulets of genius, the swirling sounds you utter.

He means this, not in a crude way, more like the permission
you give me to care for my garden-sprouts of Spring.

I nurture your hours, shield you from the passing of time,
you cannot protect me from the passing of grief. I roll

a string of sorrow into a ball and slip it inside my coat
pocket, witness the future stretch of my widowhood

to your absence. Someday, I will never see you
again. You will join the chorus of spirits in the leaves

that rustle outside our bedroom window. I anticipate
their tumble, perhaps never to return. I'll gather

the bittersweet ticking of silence into a shawl.
Oh, the cacophony of voices we now endure.

Already, rose-winged finches take your name
into their throats. One day the world will claim you,

but for now, just for now Love, I do not need
their permission—to call you, my own.

Odalisque With Raised Arms (1923)

Who am I if not the taupe off his bearded tongue,
an afterthought, something unable to land, not quite

his, not quite anyone's. If the fire from these hair
bristles stirs my larvae-tits to open like wings,

then my life begins. I was camouflaged once,
a pepper-moth drawn to a bark I could almost

disappear into, wings easily bruised by birch-birds,
a rover more certain than I. It is he who invented

this milk-pod healing — it is I who can never be cured
of it. Harem-wings poised for flight, I shall make

him just as transparent, hidden-half-hearted unable
to tread water or drown in this tulle Sargasso light.

Woman With a Hat (1905)

Fauves, I am not what you wanted. When you ogled me
wearing the sea over my head, I went silent on the canvas.
Smell me, the sweet iodine of high tide, the awkward

swirls of sea-fur and ocean kelp, drying in the sun. I am
the crooked-paste of turpentine and oil gone bad.
You want to think I am not the salt-spray on the pursed

lips of Odysseus as he struggled lashed to the mast.
He gurgled his envious sea chanteys wanting to be home.
I started as a garden, became the ocean. It was he who

silenced the sirens and not the song that silenced the sea.
Envy is a wicked man's game. My husband goes
back and forth in love and hate for his rival. He paints

mountains in the brim over my head, waterfalls, the
blue earth's breath. The tusks and scales are hidden
from the eye. They are there, all the same, the pounce

of a tufted paw. It's all inside the forest of the brain, eye-lashed,
captured: minds to the mast. They call the room where
his paintings hang a cage. But if you release us through

these bars you will notice how our skin leaves a faint
buttery talc. We are salt swirled, the callus on a conch. We are
forgotten tears drying, freckles on the face of a tiger lily.

Blue on Blue Room, Picasso's Soliloquy (1901)

Now that I have hidden you beneath prying
eyes, old friend, you continue to watch us through

cataracts, while I eliminate all traces of you.
People hidden inside fake walls have no advantage

to our scheme. One hundred years later, you won't escape
their pounce. A woman makes a fine distraction,

so it's been my experience. She soothes
her body with sponge, while your eyes weep

through the canvas, lurking to the very end. Still
you bored me with your vulgar moustache. She, the only

one of any merit, little lost raven, refused to shave
hers off. Alas the deep room smolders turquoise,

it's easy to track this scent. A coil of smoke hisses
as the paint parts, frankincense legs bruised

by plum-blush. She bends, though we know, she no longer
breathes the grey decay of air these years past. Vaporous

beard, the one I choose to brush over, ah, a voyeur
like me. Our tragic flaw, scrutiny: impossible blue-white sin.

Portrait of Gertrude Stein (1905-1906)

"The meaning of this is entirely and best to say the mark."
-Gertrude Stein

Lion, I knew because she told me that
wanted she that told me to be a lion
hooded because a lion like she wanted me
to be. Hope what is a spectacle, chair
a regular arrangement, once, I devoured her
in paint. Hooded lion, it was her exact

resemblance, exact paint was it her resembling,
I told him hooded would he like it rose, once
this so in between Harlequin resemblance exact
would like it, he. Paint unordered system to pointing
kitchen chair tight ninety times wooden she
devoured him in paint. One, he wanted a lion

and he was to be paint devoured, brown
grey broken armchair lion, sitting pouncing he eighty
or ninety times a lion wanted to be. I can't see
you any longer hooded black velvet lion
ruff hooded knew I knew once lion lingering
Chinese chair. Suggestion this was thought.

14

Three Tahitians (1899)

"I like a view but I like to sit with my back to it"
-Gertrude Stein

Vice or virtue, she nails us to the wall of a lavatory—
relegates my women to a maison pisse, my back turned

as I decide to take the apple from one or flower
from the other. Each offers paradise, our Master strokes

them with his brush, the tongue of his steady serpent.
We arouse much discussion. Captured for this moment

in ecstasy, calm and art, we are not dear like her favorites.
Money "pah"—we are elevated to a primitive Eden:

languid arms asleep in the sun. Hair: exotic water-fall,
skin: black river. We are our Master's children,

born of his coppery bristles. Confine us in the wild
dark. We pace like panthers in the pupils of their eyes.

Cezanne, Portrait of His Wife (1878)

My husband feared his father would dislike me and he did,
I have always been misunderstood by crows of ignorance.

Our business is our own; I am not so unaware of their
mean-spirited talk as I am indifferent to it. I cannot

be infiltrated by a man, even my husband hides me
behind the black tower of my eyes. He darkens my

left eye; how clever we are when we conceal what
they want; what we have. I delight in our playful

subterfuge, adorn this ebony mask of desire. I cannot give
us away the way a father gives his daughter to a dowry table.

Ever hopeful, call me star-gazer, and not Madame. Tonight,
I shall wish on all the dark-stars veiled behind blue heaven.

Rousse la Toilette (1889)

> *Three nights I sat up all night drinking absinthe, and thinking that I was singularly clear-headed and sane. The waiter came in and began watering the sawdust. The most wonderful flowers, tulips, lilies and roses, sprang up, and made a garden in the cafe. "Don't you see them?" I said to him. "Mais non, monsieur, il n'y a rien."*
> *-Oscar Wilde*

Of course I was there to talk her through,
I loved her and she loved me.

We were scattered all over the field behind
her room, madly in bloom, bursting
up half-concealed in faith, self-made —

she'd rush at me after work. I released after long hours
where I grew stronger seeking the light, all renewal,

broken up until she found me. Scattered, she joins me
to her sewing needle — my withered head,
just an achy-sweet tempered beast —

pierced through as she sings lullabies to cherubim
and I become her, soon, a small-glazed crock,

she sorts me out. I sweat, the droplets join
the bottle head, the sugar spins me soft to rest
on her tongue. I am more than a brown field barren

through the glass, emptied of flowers. My smooth neck,
all those withered moments, I cover her slick tongue,

seep through to the outside, lie down on her silky skin
in cool dirt, in blood-red slippery blossoms.

Tiger In a Tropical Storm (1891)

> *In the Real light to painting, as you did my portrait,*
> *Painting the Face of the stars.*
> *-Guillaume Apollinaire*

Each morning I walk past the lilies, the small
tigers that bare their teeth and strain towards

my waist. Here is a zoo almost in ruins,
you'd never know if it exists outside the bars

of the imagination except for the waft of piss
and moldering skins. I never give it a backward

glance nor you as you sit on a bench smoldering
inside the frets of your guitar. You are stealthy

with your songs about the garden, the tender buttons
you slip into my pockets. I could end this

at any moment, your hips straining towards
the carpel of my mouth, no one caring whether

this was risky or sweet. I remain waiting for you
for years in the weeds of your feral garden,

the forest swaggers up to us, then startles to witness
blood red lilies blooming among reedy leaves.

You pounce with fangs of fire, and me not quite
transformed, the ground scrapes against my back.

I am not changed into raindrops in sky
or black-freckled petals. You are just another

ordinary tiger unable to devour us in flames.

Little Dancer of Fourteen Years (1881)

You look ridiculous if you dance
You look ridiculous if you don't dance
So you might as well dance.
-Gertrude Stein

You won't know me by my name, Marie Van Goethem,
and that is another secret I shall not rush to whisper,
but this I shall say: the 6 Francs earned sitting for him,
provided luxuries for my sisters and me. Sweet cake icing

is my downfall. The swirls remind me of virgin snow
that paint the streets pure. Afterwards, when money
becomes hard to earn in an honorable way, I borrow
700 Francs from a stupidly drunk customer

and get caught. Juliet? I was your age last year, before I knew
better, Foolish Heart. Your stars scatter across the sky.
You and your beloved melt on my tongue. Now I am older
and know never to trust moon wishes that fall as cold stars.

Inside Alice B. Toklas

Remember: If perfection is good, more perfection is better.
                                                        Alice B. Toklas

Treacherous floods of gooey and pungent thoughts,
like a soothsayer of wild-winged poems: I know
all things. Naturally, there lives a stout woman inside,
me trying to get out. Out a stout woman inside, a rose
repeat, a rose repeat, a fat bumble bee'd black
mustachioed rose vainly, insanely scrambling to get out.
Alice B. Toklas me, neither took life easy nor fraternized
casually. Come out, Thorny weather and will you not come out?

In between stormy black petals, sparks my lips a bee,
a bumbler: oui. I cook, I smolder, seduce the fatty broth
of genius. She, takes all my time. Haschich fudge, licked
from my lips. I make life off a genius, in between, I suffocate
pigeons—*Coo coo*, forever beaucoup, le petite mort: Ja, du.
The throb as fingers stroke the throaty murmuring, murdering
generation, for better purpose, lost. The drum, the hum,
the Hem, the men. Carp to murder,

those awful braying Barbaries, the plucky twist of thunder,
the turning of a screw, bill first then coo, a man's nuts,
the phallic necks of chickens—better to wring than cut. Out,
out brief genius fire, husband—lyre, out. We summon them
by coal wild-fire eyes. The paint bristles of my lips. They all
want what we have. Coo, violet bird—coo dove, vagina dentata,
rose is rose, ich, du. Whistle her slave, vagrant-master, mistress—
knave. Schatzchen, ni moi sans vous, Liebster, ni moi sans vous.

Hem Party

Hemingway's remarks are not literature. Gertrude Stein

While visiting, I attempted to complete one true sentence,
one brave phrase that would last. The skinny one
muttered while she hacked the thorny long stems I brought

"rose is a rose is a rose." Meanwhile, I whetted my hacker,
waited for the Husbands to arrive. I was informed I was

inaccroachable, a phrase, that wolves used, that wild boars
salivated over. That blasted sentence, would it never appear?
I tried to keep it clean, my truest, unmarred diction. I tried

summoning it by suggesting all sentences weren't whores.
The Wife told me, I was naïve. She said I was white and horny.
She minced no words, ravished the wild air with her

kitchen knife. She punctuated our silence with little bursts
of praise for her Husband. She didn't like me; she glowered,

sulked. Asked me three times if I were staying for supper.
Finally I responded: "depends, what is on the menu?" A sly grin
formed "cockles, one of Pusses little fetishes. A-live a-live, oh!"

Oh, I said I would pass, what were these two on about? Finally,
finally, I had started dressing my buck-naked, bare as bones

sentence. I had made a randy start. Picasso arrived, the dark one
said "We'll send you both home satisfied, with mussels.
Don't worry. Our picnics are delish. You do enjoy cheesy

accoutrements, little nibbles? Garlands in the dark. You'll have
a bit of succulent tongue, won't you? Please try my fudge."

What Ezra Thought

I grope in the mass of lies, knowing most
of the sources are wholly untrustworthy.
  Ezra Pound, a Village Explainer (Gertrude Stein)

Let me go on record, I dislike them. I hate
their dogs, her name is the vessel for crude

brew, and God help them they are unfortunate
in their looks. One is a shadow of the Other,

and needs a good shave. The Other can't be
pinched into a decent shoe or girdle.

They are niggardly with money. They worship
daft pieces of art, and they don't spend

on furnishings. Each time I go there,
I break something: everything is paste and faux

wood, their dildos are probably glue and brick.
Yes, they say they are in love. Pah, right down

to their crooked nose hair, their chin whiskers,
even their yappy dogs and frumpy cars are more

feminine, less mannequin hard, with faces like
a handmade pipe, all black scowl and fumes.

What Estlin Thought

I should have lived in China, where a poet is also a painter.
e.e. cummings

Another tomorrow, hence, Gertrude Stein will be all
the rage, all, her friend (s), a little calligraphy rose

forgotten, black painted edge(s) their bodies, fire (+)
ash, shadow-poems, one larger than and the other

scurrying feet & canvas, their moustaches quiver
like a mouse anticipating puss. Tails, rice-teeth, past

captured ink, they have made mad-dog poets flail, While e e
absorbs strokes/? their sclerotic welts of paint, their black

tubes, their black black chatter sticks of oily chalk, talk-
pastels, India-ink, their chocolate lips += Noon-English mad.

La nuit dernière au salon

The paintings are our children, I suppose;
At times, perhaps, the painters are as well.
To feed, to love, to see how talent grows.

The Spaniard let us underwrite his shows—
And his success was easy to foretell.
The paintings were our children, I suppose.

He often brought us guests, but never foes.
A stranger bleeding paint, Le Tour Eiffel—
When fed and loved a talent quickly grows.

A feast of Braques, Picassos and Rousseaus—
Their gardens wet with paint and fine pastel.
The painters were our children, I suppose.

The wives of genius: rose is rose is rose.
My little Pussy cat was uber Belle.
To feed, to love, to see how talent grows.

To part with one the bitterest of blows—
like giving up an artery to sell.
To feed, to love, to see how talent grows.
The paintings were our children, I suppose.

PART II – Other Legends

Venus and Mary

It's easy to say without her arms, she is tormented,
just like the maids who have no legs, but what have they

exchanged love for, what virtue has been denied?
The hole beneath her breast is the same wound

that the beggar Mary has, eyes fevered with Jesus.
I met her once, years ago, on the streets of Jerusalem.

Mary, like Venus, is beautiful even with her broken
nose, her peasant's legs. Despite the fact there

are no fingers to worry the scars that God has left,
the loss was always just below the longing; I suspect

mermaids and spirits have this in common.
Tears pour down their cheeks, one marble, one flesh.

You might say a marble flower cannot spring up
from the sea like a wild coral bird, still every woman

has her own story. Mary, Venus, even the absent
arms are white as clouds. They were unable

to take a man to their breast, to pat them, to say
"there, there." The ghost of the sound of waves lapping

on marble skin, the sound of a bell in a decaying ark.
Inside them, all women carry the sea.

The Statue Hermione

For these last few hours, I will lie quietly,
among the smoke of bones and memories

that were left in mirrors and brought back
to me, spiraling down off the tips of owls,

of angel wings. I would kneel if I were able
to have my flesh back—not this alabaster truss.

The wind howls around me, the cries of all human
flesh release the skin of the other: love-making,

angels and sheep stir in the grass, I suppose
you know we never fully sleep because of prey.

I suppose you will say I was sixteen years gone,
this is why my fevers left. I chose to keep

the company of women, men with their salty tongues,
spewing out the stuff that produces urchins, seas

and seeds along with pools of lies. I became a statue
brought back to life to make the rest

of a conjuror's days. Pity me now my skin
so touched, my former life so clean and cold.

Walking with Emily Bronte

To fall in love you need to be willing
to believe in ghosts and to know
the wild perfume of the implacable beast,
the insouciance of the untamed girl.

Words have scents like flowers.
Honeysuckle and harebell, desire trailed
me and in his madness threw me
from a cliff. I wander the high fells

neither to conjure up his drowsy shade
nor to perish alone in the fierce tempest
of love, but to once again go out gathering
garlands of moonbeams or lightning.

The Ghost of Branwell Drinks Bitter at the Black Bull

Everyone loves a good story, so here's mine.
You'll say I am barking but not so moony I don't know
what I am. Their litanies could make another poem

altogether. She repeated, more than once, I was the smartest
man she'd known, and then she turned cold. No,

not in death, she wouldn't look me in the eyes, she sent me
home. How could I face them? Charlotte haranguing me to fix
myself clean. Em, almost gone, traipsing the moors,

befriending rabbits and turnips: half-seducing ghosts.
They called me a broken fence, useless even to animals.

I thought of bulrushes snapping their swords, turtles and trees
talking back. Brambles snaked my ankles, thistle bound me to all
those "what ifs" and "what fors." If she'd only been a whore.

Was I rooted to this place a cracked jug without a cork,
no means to grow my life back, no bottle to shine

my eyes amber, to make me glow for her? After she refused
the sight of me, or any apology I could make, she cast me
back to my own kind. It was then I took to sucking her glass

lips, her cold indifferent tits. After too many days of this,
I confess I had my old legs back. And then the Reverend

appeared. See how he glowers at me, in the corner of this place?
Lip curled, he insists on my charity, my temperance
to forgive them all. I promised my sisters I would take none

of the bad, just enough to loosen the buttons of my trousers,
to take her legs around my waist, that frock spilled wild

across the chair. It is time now for me to return to my rest.
Another March will summon him to me, each to
the other. He, who shot his seed like a rifle into my cunt-mother.

Maybe, this year, tonight, he'll nod his acceptance my way.
Maybe his lips will brush warm on mine. Forgive me

Father, just this once for I have sinned. But what worth
is a man without a kind lady who cried out
I was made of the softest deerskin cape, the nights she undressed

for me? The amber moon averted its eyes, placing bread
on our willing tongues, giving us peace and its blessing, finally.

Living in the Body of a Horsefly
Haematopota pluvialis

Some call me common, yet I recall those who did more than
chew on the skin of their rivals, the ones who became greater
than an irritant lapping another poet's blood. I have been around
a while. My uncles in the past had lineage, not to be sexist, aunts

too, yet it was the Uncles who raced on the rumps of the chariots,
whose lives were driven short by the whip with their dizzy
bursts of glory as they watched the dolphin counters, knowing
their mere participation could change the course of history.

Not to be a name dropper, but my family lived in the stables
of the Lord and Lady of Coventry. In fact, it was "Tom" her
groom, who invited us to stay, and we took the utmost care never
to mar her skin, what a beauty she was, so kind. The vulgars

gossiped she was hot to trot, who would blame her, given
that stingy galoot she married. Our family members
had stellar careers. My immediate situation, however,
was a step down, not a leg up. Some rogues stowed

on the Mayflower; we Loyalists chose to propagate Jolly Olde.
Racing was permanently in our blood. King George VI Weekend
remains a highlight for us each Summer. Call me traditional,
but that sense of duty, and of course family nagged us

throughout the centuries. Legends have passed down from the
first time Great Aunt Margaret heard them in that old-world
stable. Those divine times, (circumstances that we were cautioned
to keep silent about). Yet, repeated by a man who liked men

(and sometimes women) who with the heady ghosts of my elders
was never common: "whose spirit with divine ambition puff'd."

Washing Godiva's Hair

A pattern along the covered bricks becomes hers,
and all the other things I know she loves: the names
of birds—brown Juliet capped chicks, black-tufted
tits. Then along our walk because I am surely there
beside her with my unseen hands, pushing into
the plaits of her then braided hair, counting each knot
as if it were a rosary bead. Someone has to wash
her hair, wring out the lemon water or rose petals.

I have lain in thinking of all those languages.
The honeyed trail of words that drips her name down
and through the thick air. God comes first, always
or I'll fall to my knees, repenting, then the beginning
of our places: ivy, I say "ah" while I wring out her length.
The drapes that don't reveal or conceal, a bee that suckles,
then the walk, the Rose of Sharon, impatiens—
she is mine and I am responsible and happy to aid her
as we avoid the tyranny of men, of tax.

Icarus Plays Atlantic City

When I was no more than ten, my mother dressed me up
in feathers. It wasn't exotic; we were pragmatic and found
woodland browns and greens, no peacock ravished me,

no swan had his way. But she told me "without facts
there cannot be faith" and I knew I was gifted.
And so I practice, along with the horses, to dive

off a cliff. I know you have seen that act. Horribly,
in the 20's a girl was blinded! For me, it is practice,
practice, practice. One day I will be ready

for Carnegie Hall. In between, I do stand-up.
It is odd to see a man adorned with feathers.
Like a cross-dressing flamingo, hitch-hiking my way

across the U.S.A., I do a damned good Lou Reed.
Moon-fogged after 2 A.M. Mom and I spread
feathers around the room. Woodpeckers with polka-dot

ties make the best ascots. Imagine a spread
of seahorse pink, moss-green and violet:
smoky as an angel's wings. Some say my sister

stepped on an asp (others that a handful of pills
did her in). In the back room she WAS everybody's
darlin'. Oh, those gold brachile she wore with such grace.

Soon I will be ready to leap with those horses and set
those strange angels spinning. We will neigh, fly towards
a perfect marigold sun, dive down through fingers of salt.

The Birds that Lay Down for Icarus

Cormorants conspire to peck each other
to death to furnish him with wings.

Owls call in the sleep of trees.
Huddled together after a night of sex,
their wings ripple patterns in sand.

Larks rise earlier than usual,
throw themselves against weathered wood.
The old man walking out in the blue morning
finds a hundred still birds, a trail
of blood outside windows and doors.

He gives thanks for the ease of his prophecy.
The old man settles to pluck at faith—
to tell his son of their good fortune.

In days, fields are no longer
littered with bodies. The air ripples
with a silence like bird song.

Sappho receives a note from the lover
of Icarus warning her against flights
off cliffs. The envelope is sealed with wax
hardened by cold tears. She offers a feather
crusty from sea spray and blood.

Two Doves, Dorothy and William Wordsworth

STAY near me—do not take thy flight!
A little longer stay in sight! William Wordsworth

I would have made a bad mother, you said. Shuttered
milk eyes, the way I search for white deer

where there are none. I saw one once, a freak
of nature, a ghost or a symbol of some other god,

one I was sure to be jealous of. You said so many things,
I could not love. We had two wash basins side by side,

"renew thyself," you said. And the thought of cleansing
my body so close to yours, within minutes of that pass;

all I could think was the sponging off, the tinkling of water
against skin like wind chimes, never to be put into a breath

or a thought. The roof, at this time, housed a family of doves
and they taunted me, cooing and brooding overhead, scratching

and clawing on the roof. What did they want, I wondered?
If they wanted peace, I wanted them to be different

like the white deer. I wanted them to raise their family
and shove off, leave us to our business. I think I wanted

to be an inky bat, waiting to creep the bedcovers, waiting
to steal your breath. Poised as I was to write it all down, leave

my own bloody mark. I wanted to suckle your blood, snatch flies
from the air. All women want to eat their babies, I told you.

You will say I have imagined this when our affection
is pure. I think that my journal is not free enough to talk.

Perhaps the sponge and water know the truth of it.
When I put my nose to the crumbs of skin, when I bring

the fountain of you out to the garden, the worms,
the ready earth, are thirsty for what we have.

War, Joan of Arc
for Guy Des Rosiers

For nothing in the world will I swear not to arm
myself and put on a man's dress; I must obey
the orders of Our Lord. Joan of Arc

He draws the Knight of Swords: a youth of twenty years stares
through fire. They are in a gallery of ghosts, a museum
of sorrow and desire. She sees him through a mirror, looks past

to the other side. A crimson veil rises down the bright corridor
of poppies. She is freed of her prison of skin, she is beyond
touch, beyond the bony fang of the moon. She is beyond

all thoughts real and imagined. Afterwards, she bursts into flight
as a cardinal on dangerous wings. Her entrails slither
away like a coral snake, when you kissed her, it was the barbed

red tongue of the devil. In your final vision, you see her
as sharp swords among red winter berries. She is the crackle
of bone in a flame colored tunic.

Death
for John Connell

The Charles River looked inviting during that March thaw, but
I found myself ambivalent to its beauty, wondering if you are dead
in that way were you cold or did all creature comforts vanish. Smoke

into a starry night, after a gunshot, or as Mitchell put it "one minute
a candle flame, then out." Not that he was the first to suggest this.
Visiting him that year, after his sick heart rested, we had lots of these

conversations. He was not a believer in an afterlife, I was. We argue
we always have, how he trusts me with a pen, even in this poem,
is a miracle. He will say it is inaccurate. He likes Emily Dickinson.

I dislike her tiny yelps and gasps. I defend the merit of Whitman's
line, long and flowing, like a river. We argue all day and sometimes
late into the night. But this day, a day like any other except, I walked

further than usual, too far in fact, I found myself ready for a rest.
Which is why when the carriage stopped, a driver waving me inside
I entered, almost like a sleep walker, I entered and sat down.

Sitting before me, was Mr. Death himself, his bony knees knocking
against mine like castanets. Reader, he was not blue-eyed like Mr.
Estlin declared once, his eyes were sherry-colored, warm, inviting

almost. Not like that damned river, I have seen those eyes too,
icy blue 20 degrees Fahrenheit, like my father's in fact, but I swear
on the sake of poetry, his were brown. He was impeccably dressed,

a dandy almost, and well accessorized, yes he had a hat. Robert
Graham shirt, argyle socks, you'd be happy to know, he was no
conservative dresser. Tired as I was I slapped the driver's door,

said "I'll just as soon walk" and left that confined box, burst out
like a silver Charles River fish heading for a waterfall. Afterwards,
when I tell this story, while Mitchell argues the merits of Emily,

I tell him he has on the same pair of socks as I saw in the carriage.
I watch him remove each sock, although it is winter, and throw
them out the window. He tells me there's a fly buzzing, swats it,

says he doesn't know how it survived the winter, and to finish
my tea. Later we'll go back to the river, I'll show him the carriage,
beg him for another ride. He swears I've been blessed and cursed.

Famine, Persephone
for Keith Talbot

Our skin was black like an oven because of the terrible famine.
Lamentations

To the Empress, drawn and red, I say, I shall never write to you
again. Lost Mother, I have put so much distance between us,

I do not want to be found. The forest floor is littered with leaves.
In Winter wind, I am a guest here, one vagrant husk among
the others. I wake on a bed of nettles, my hand over the place

of grief in my body. Any protection these small hands offer
is useless. I am unable to attach a runaway leaf to a tree.

The Sister of Lazarus Leaves Cyprus

When I wake, it is in a forest, different
from the Island where we live. I plant
a fig tree to remind me of home.
At the end of my longing is a door

to release me to sorrow. All journeys
begin with a false footstep.
Overhead, branches shift, creaking
in the wind. I am alone for the first time

from the center of my life. Fearful birds
dart, shadow-mice skitter into deeper forest.
Whatever is left of his starry voice,
let me hear it before it is taken by the night.

I loved a man who was born twice to a passion
I cannot stir with my hands.
Let me lie under these trees that glow
with eyes but conceal moonlight. Let me pray

for a distance that lets me stop counting
figs on a tree not accustomed to change.

Sappho and the Painter

Last night, I couldn't sleep
for watching you paint me,
the whorls of hair on your wrists,
electric.

They will wonder if we are the same.
They will gather feathers for my flight
off the abyss. I have letters
from the maid of Icarus—we know
how that recklessness ended.
She waited in the sea-foam below
his feet, content in their promises to meet.

Promises are sea shells spent
in a raging sea. I am no less
a woman for falling
in love with a soul,
be it phallus or delta.

Pleasure is pleasure, simply put.
Wise Circe and her swine-men.
I take a flower to my lips to taste honey.
Have you ever licked your fingers after
devouring a peach? Whether the juice
running down your chin is fruit
or your own—pleasure
is pleasure, I repeat.

My painter captures me perfectly, but for that—
my orchid-black eyes, my love-sleep forest fur,
the mystery will always be:
is my love a he,
or a woman like me.

To Sleep With Keats

And seal the hushed casket of my soul.

The train that brings me to him has a snoot full of diesel,
which reminds me of a snood that I am wearing on my hair.
My mother would know, but John is dying, who cares about

words? He's already dead by some accounts, this city bile rising
in his throat. We are in Rome, I am thumbing through his pages.

I am touching his fever, laying my hands on his face like fronds.
I am the doctor sent to cure him, I am sitting on the edge
of his cot pleading with worms and blades, trying to bleed him.

I am his final miracle, I am the one who will coax him back to life
with each piss-colored pass of broth to his lips. His lungs rise

like a porridge that scalds the stove, bubbling down the front
of his chest. John is half dead. I am distressed. He rasps, pleads
in fits and starts, her name bubbling blood on his lips. I tell him

to tell me plain. His friend waits for me in the museum, heart
throbbing under the floorboards. I want to know which woman

did them in? I lay my head on his chest, he begs for laudanum,
thinks I am Fanny. The museum closes in 25 minutes, but I am
reading him To Sleep. He tells me there's coin in his purse, to help

myself. He tells me his pocket watch is ticking past the museum's
closing, to not fret over him, to give Percy his best regards.

Fanny Godwin and the Monster

Did I solicit thee from darkness to promote me?
Milton, *Paradise Lost*

It's like an old story. I am already gone. I tunnel
through the dark while our father conjures
filth around me. Mary huddles before their bonfire,
dreaming of her freak. And every day they go
sailing on wine-dark waters. In gibberish I plead,
release me, like a fish into those seas you cannot fathom.
She pieces together skin and sparks that crackle lightning,
that split the forests of Darwin. Impenetrable to love

I slip through the slender ribs of the world. I sew
a scrap of nightmare, paste sloppy edges
to my sister's stars. I have already crossed over.
She stitches her baby from black-forest skin.
The wolves of summer spill deep into the forest.
I spin light through glass, messages through their planchette.
A promise of oppressive love may soak through
their sticks: I announce myself to him. My lover
is a poppy, her lover is a lightning storm. As my sister
carries angels, I force words through their crystal glass.
My baby's cry wakes me in the night. I suckle
failure. I knit him from shredded petals.

An Ocean as a Deity

Fear not for the future, weep not for the past.
  Percy Bysshe Shelley

At night, the white caps I feared are pillows
to rest my head upon. I am content
to talk with souls who spent nine months floating
in the dark sea of Mary. Don Juan
is no ladies' ship splintered by romance.
These years have made me fitful with visions.
A child claps like a naked deity while friends
bloody and mangled, arrive to report my house
is falling down. This womb is crowded with weeds.
Mary will laugh to learn how I stayed alive lecturing
God about my unborn children. A fishnet will drag
me to the sands of Lerici where my heart will beat
until she finds me. It drums as steady in a gull's mouth
as in my wife's hands, when she returns it to me.

Ophelia Rises from Her Stream

My groom deceived us all, this much is certain, he was the cold
fingers of water that lulled me drowsy and now awake.

I rest on a pillow named remembrance, rosemary is what
they said, what dreams I had while fish wove their tendrils

of weed. I find twice I've been deceived. Death is not freeing,
it leaves me cold forever. Lilies wrap me like a maid's corset.

I remain unwed to the haughty breeze, only to dragonflies, to
the drowsy turtles with their *loves me not*. My groom will weep,

while they fill my purse with carp, not gold I can spend
on the street. Meanwhile, my beloved speaks to skulls, writes

verses to flowerpots, to bony ginger jars that hold no thought.
We are forever writing poetry inside the sleeves of the dead.

I said all the pansies were faces of children planning their escape.
My father, my brother made no such deal for me. I have flitted

before them at the gate, in lavender veils, in webbed wings.
They tuck me to bed inside their watery jars. I am terminally

in green, the majesty of being Queen to all these flowers. Imagine
the garlands that will corrupt my head in paint? I rule all my frogs:

real princes and imagined with their ermine capes of froth. Oh,
the lullabies of my sweet stream. What better bridegroom this,

Dear Father, let me be gone. When the moonlight catches
my hair and turns me into mist, I walk from stone to silent stone.

Tapestry

First she gave me her loom, Goddess and human,
we each went to work. What can I tell you about
her that you don't already know? She silenced

them into believing that hers was brightest, she knew
many Gods and some gave up their wares, acorns
were mashed into dyes, birds sweetly molted their

blues and greens for her. She conjured each trick
while I, with no magic, wove. Then she said:
"Behold this world Father has created. These rivers

churn silver and gold, these trees drip diamond raindrops.
Now, Father is a man who doesn't skimp in his abundance.
I sprang from his brain fully armored and ready

to take on this world with no thought of women's pleasures."
Which leaves me, not a Goddess, trapped at my loom,
creating a life in my tapestry. As her colors spill out and she

reveals herself to us, the dusty road she travels, the burning
bed she falls into exhausted each night, I am forced
to live an ordinary life. These luminescent threads call me

back to myself, weaving me and binding me into my own
spidery world, yet she is the one to whom the frogs call out
their strange vowels, summoning her further from the city.

Summary Garden

after Anna Akhmatova

I want to see the roses
in the park
where I played as young
as the newly formed statues there.

Rain drops
tiptoe in puddles
that grow as we splash.
We wade through pools
of uncertain dreams.
We swim in lonely desire.

I see their chiseled bodies
with unblinking eyes
regard me
a pink, imperfect bud.

I imagine them now
moss laureled halos
mother-of-pearl and shell
and I wonder if they still
tend the roses
whether they are too old now,
whether I am too old.
And what of their loneliness?
And what of mine?

The Wild Fir

You appeared to me, your face
a green filigree, like the fancy willow plates
my great aunt coveted until the last one broke
before her marriage. I decided you were not able
to touch me in a personal way. And yet
you protected me when I used you for shelter,

tying my laces when I skated the pond and gusting
needles of ice came from every direction. I have bored
every lover with this; I am needier than other
people. The absence of moaning left us both
shaken when the taps at our window were a nagging
branch or a runaway cone distracting me

from coming. I am alone now, you have ruined
another good thing, another chance of happiness.
I am the last of the romantics: bury me under
the blanket of your boughs, the thick bristles
of solstice fir a bed for me to crawl though
as I did in my former life, the one without you.

ABOUT THE AUTHOR

Laurie Byro's first poetry collection, *Luna*, was published in 2015 from Aldrich Press and her chapbook *Wonder* is forthcoming from Little Lantern Press. Her poetry has been published in a wide range of venues, including university presses, online journals, anthologies, and a grade-school textbook. She has received frequent honors in Web del Sol's InterBoard Poetry competitions; in January 2011 she was named one of the IBPC "Poets of the Decade" for garnering the highest number of awards of all competing poets in the decade ending 2010.

.

www.ingramcontent.com/pod-product-compliance
Lightning Source LLC
Chambersburg PA
CBHW072051040426
42447CB00012BB/3091